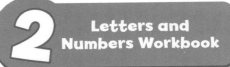

2 Letters and Numbers Workbook

T0268558

⭕ Trace. ✏ Write. 🖍 Color.

Present the letter. Then the children trace and write the letters with different colored crayons. Finally, they color the apple freely.

⭕ Trace. ✏️ Write. 🖌️ Paint.

Present the letter. Then the children trace and write the letters with different colored crayons. Finally, they finger-paint the letter and the bananas. Alternatively, children the can color the letter and the bananas with crayons.

⭕ Trace. ✏️ Write. ✏️ Color.

Present the letter. Then the children trace and write the letters with different colored crayons. Finally, they color the cat and letter freely.

C   c   c   c   c   c   c

C

✋ Count. ◯ Trace. ✏ Color.

Present the numbers. The children name the objects and count them. Then they trace the numbers with different colored crayons. Finally, the children color the objects freely.

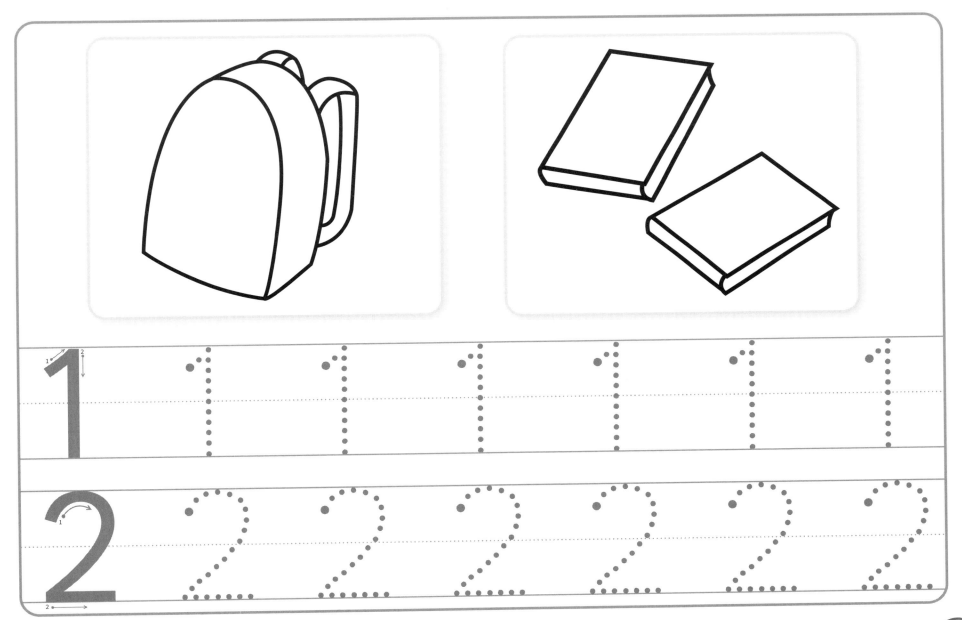

 **Count.** **Trace.** **Color.**

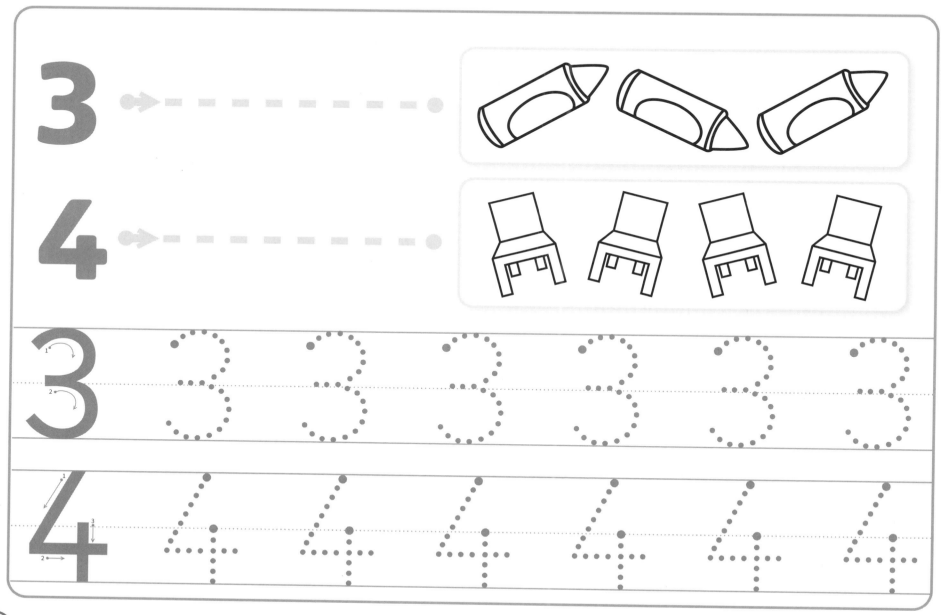

 **Count.** ◯ **Trace.** ✏ **Color.**

Present the numbers. Then the children count the frogs and trace the number 5. Repeat the procedure for the flowers and the number 6. Finally, the children color the frogs and the flowers.

✏️ **Color.** ⭕ **Trace.** ✏️ **Write.**

Present the letter. Then the children color the pictures for the words that start with the letter "d." Finally, they trace and write the letters with different colored crayons.

daddy **dog** **apple**

 **Color.** ⚪ **Trace.** ✏ **Write.**

Present the letter. Then the children look at the letters in the box and color the letters "e." Finally, they trace and write the letters with different colored crayons.

✏️ Color. ⭕ Trace. ✏️ Write.

 Present the letter. Then the children find the letters "f" in the picture and color the corresponding sections. Finally, they trace and write the letters with different colored crayons.

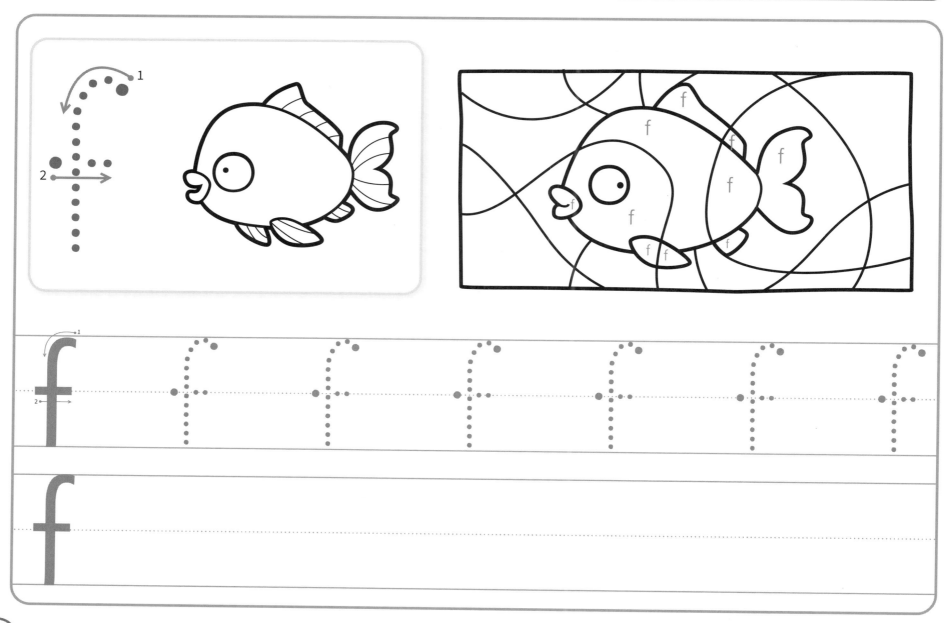

 Count. ◯ Trace. ✏ Color.

 Present the numbers. Then the children count the circles in each number and trace the numbers with different colored crayons. Finally, they color the circles in the numbers.

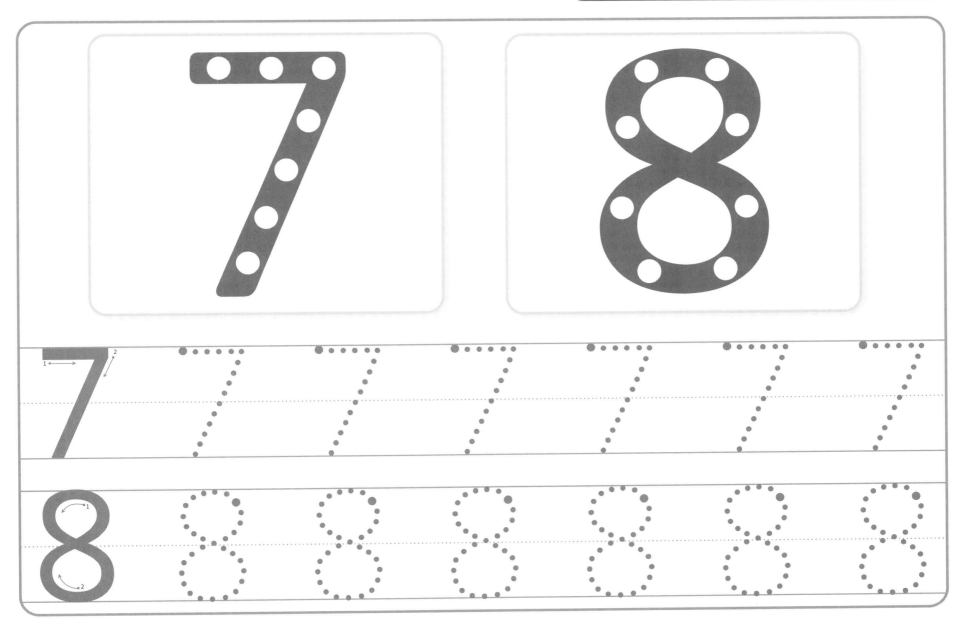

 **Draw.** **Trace.** **Write.**

 **Count.** ⭕ **Trace.** ✏️ **Color.**

Unit 3

⭕ **Trace.** ✏️ **Write.** ✏️ **Color.**

Present the letter. Then the children trace and write the letters with different colored crayons. Finally, they color the gorilla freely.

◯ Trace. ✏ Write. 🖌 Paint.

Present the letter. Then the children trace and write the letters with different colored crayons. Finally, they finger-paint the letter and the hat. Alternatively, the children can color the letter and the hat with crayons.

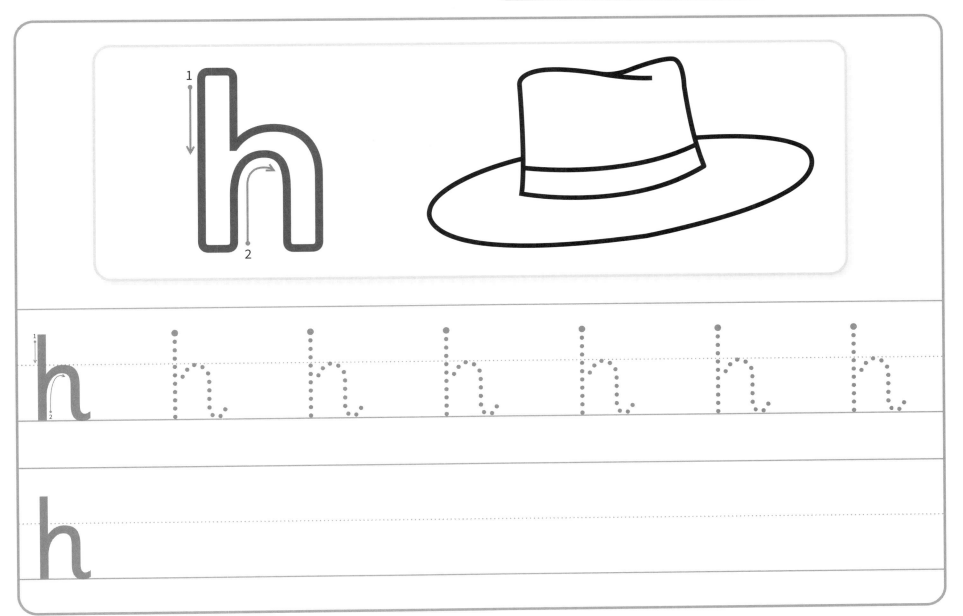

⭕ Trace. ✏ Write. ✏ Color.

Present the letter. Next, the children trace and write the letters with different colored crayons. Finally, they color the letter and the igloo freely.

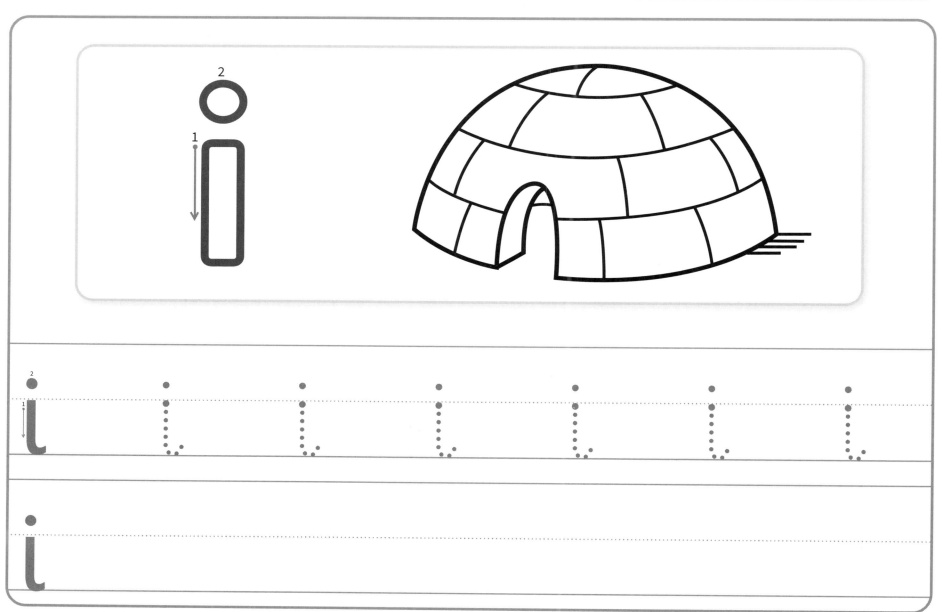

 **Count.** **Trace.** **Color.**

 Present the number. Then the children count the toy cars and trace the numbers with different colored crayons. Finally, they color the cars freely.

 **Count.** **Trace.** ✏ **Color.**

✋ Count. ◯ Circle. ◯ Trace. ✏ Color.

The children count the dolls and circle the corresponding number. Repeat the same procedure for the balls. Then they trace the numbers with different colored crayons. Finally, the children color the pictures freely.

11 12

11 12

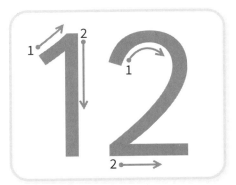

12

12 12 12 12 12 12 12 12

 **Color.** **Trace.** **Write.**

Present the letter. Then the children color the pictures of the words that start with the letter "j". Finally, they trace and write the letters with different colored crayons.

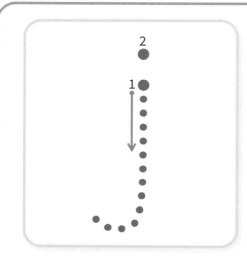

 **jacket**

hat

 **juice**

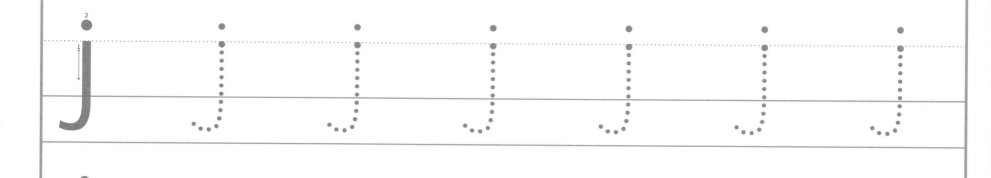

j

j

 **Color.** ◯ **Trace.** ✏ **Write.**

Present the letter. Then the children identify and color the letters "k" in the box. Finally, they trace and write the letters with different colored crayons.

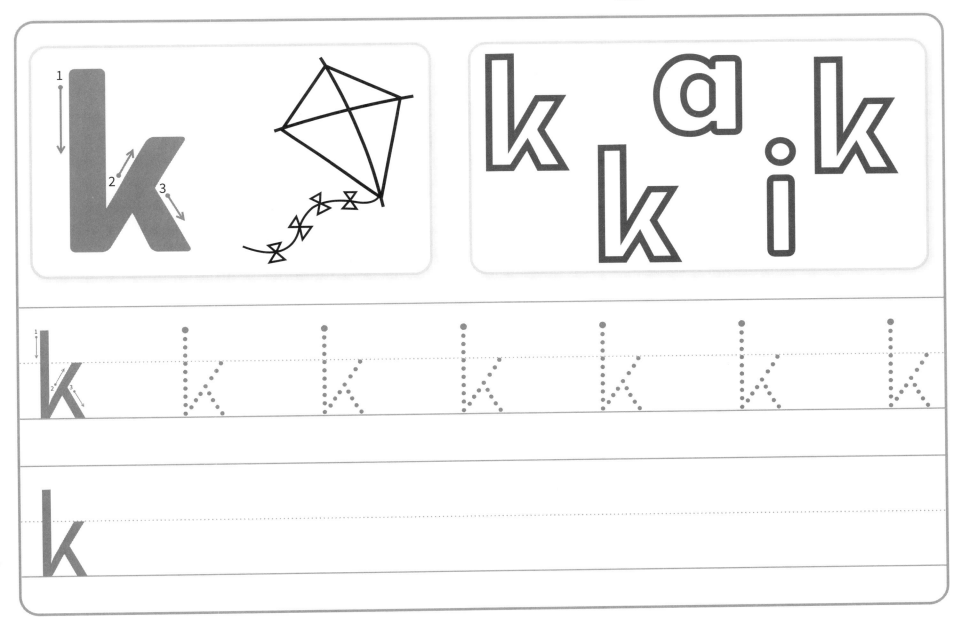

Trace. ✏ Write. 🖍 Color.

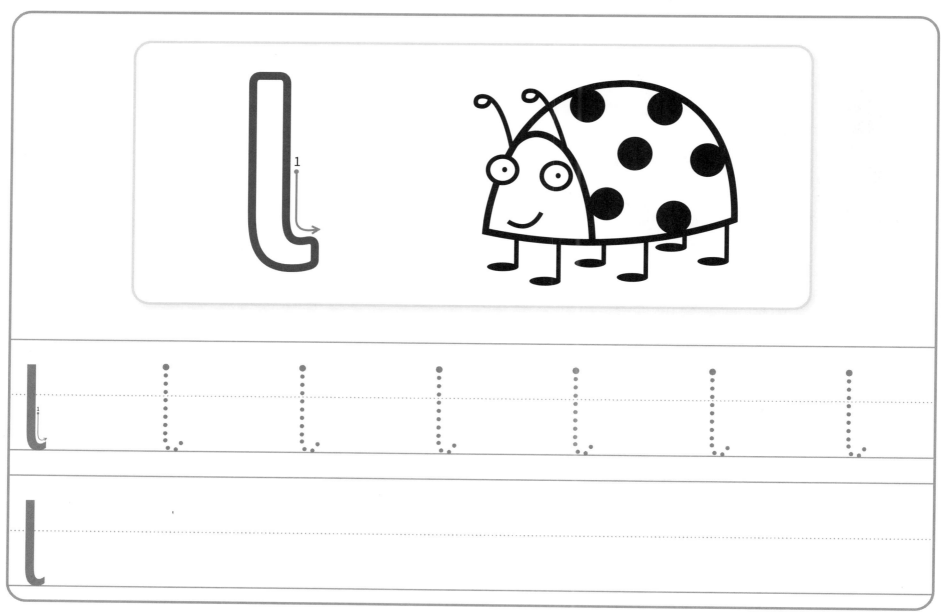

 Count. ⬡ Trace. ✏ Color.

Present the number. Then the children count the heads and trace the numbers with different colored crayons. Finally, they color the heads freely.

 **Count.** ⬭ **Trace.** ✏ **Color.**

 **Count.** **Trace.** **Color.**

Review the numbers. Then the children count the fish and the cats and trace the numbers with different colored crayons. Finally, they color the pictures freely.

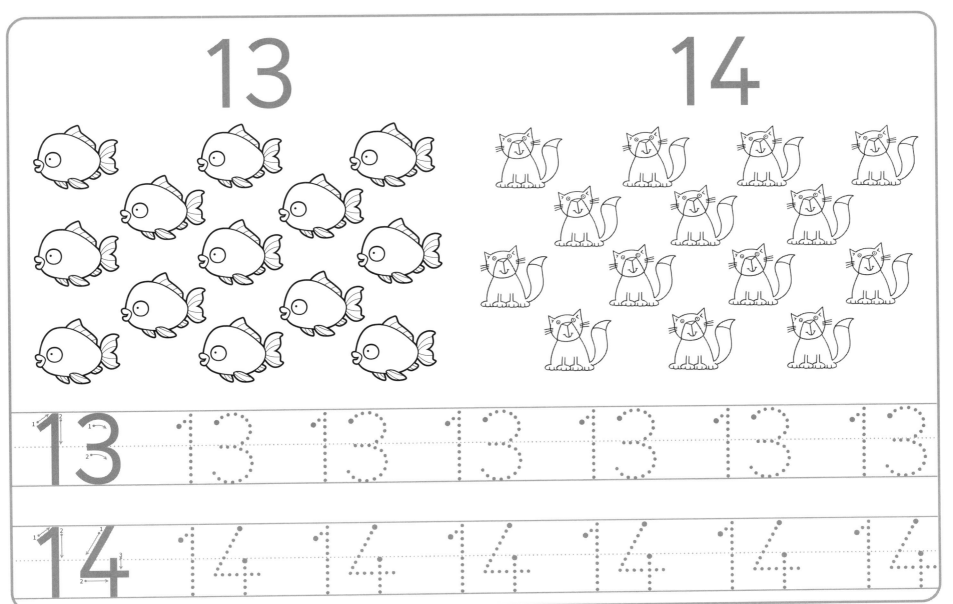

13

14

13 13 13 13 13 13 13

14 14 14 14 14 14 14

Unit 5

⭕ **Trace.** ✏️ **Write.** 🖍️ **Color.**

m m m m m m m m m

m

⭕ Trace. ✏️ Write. 🖌️ Paint.

Present the letter. Then the children trace and write the letters with different colored crayons. Finally, they finger-paint the letter "n" and the neck. Alternatively, the children can color the letter and the neck with crayons.

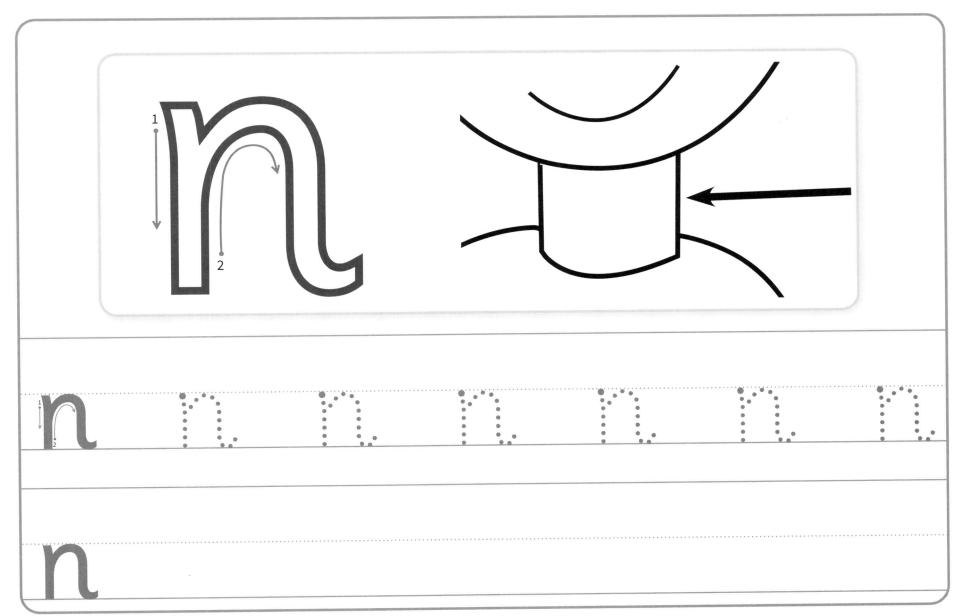

◯ Trace. ✎ Write. ✎ Color.

Present the letter. Then the children trace and write the letters with different colored crayons. Finally, they color the letter and the octopus freely.

 **Follow.** **Draw.**

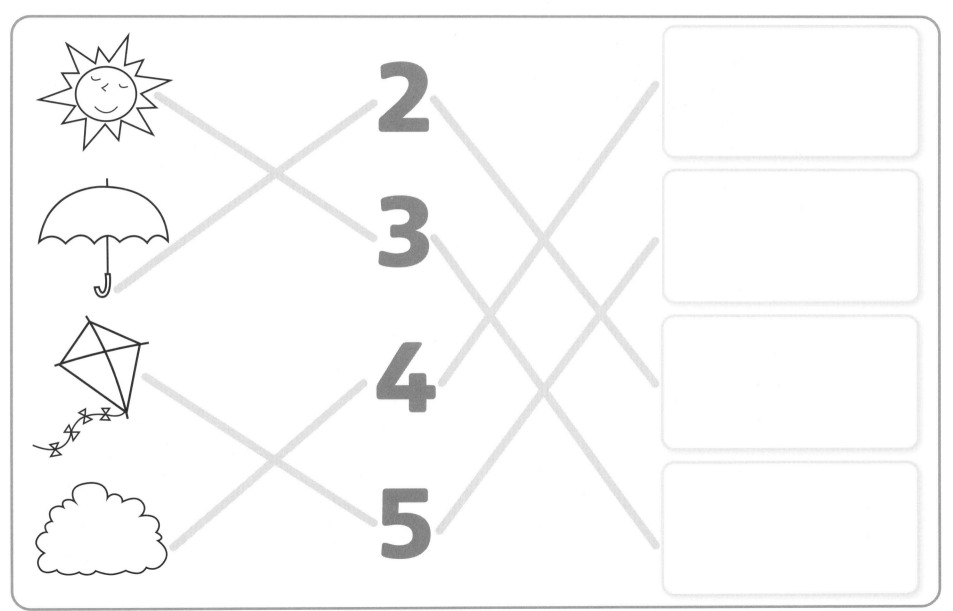

✋ Count. ○ Circle.

6   7

8   7

9   7

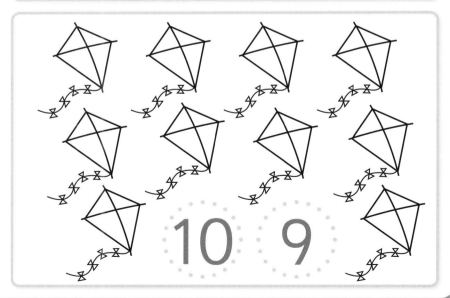

10   9

 **Trace.** **Draw.**

Unit 6

✏️ **Color.** ⭕ **Trace.** ✏️ **Write.**

Present the letter. Then the children color the pictures of the words that start with the letter "p." Finally, they trace and write the letters with different colored crayons.

pen

mouse

pencil

p   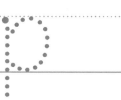

p

 **Color.** ◯ **Trace.** ✎ **Write.**

 Present the letter. The children identify the letters "q" and color them. Then they color the queen. Finally, they trace and write the letters with different colored crayons.

 # Color. ◯ Trace. ✎ Write.

 Present the letter. Then the children find the letters "r" in the picture and color the corresponding sections. Finally, they trace and write the letters with different colored crayons.

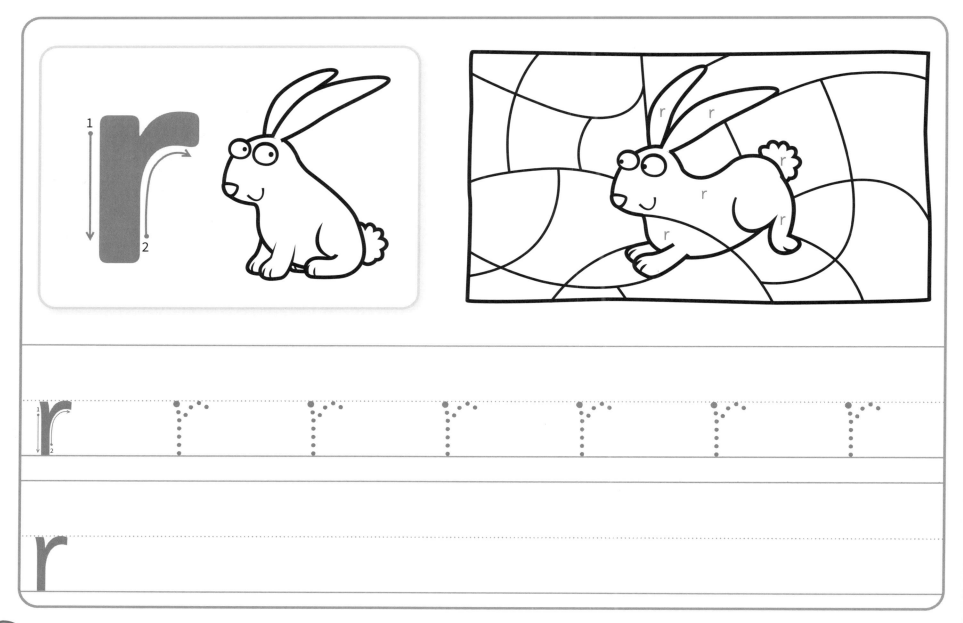

 **Count.** ○ **Trace.** ✏ **Color.**

 Present the number. Then the children count the cows and trace the numbers with different colored crayons. Finally, they color the cows freely.

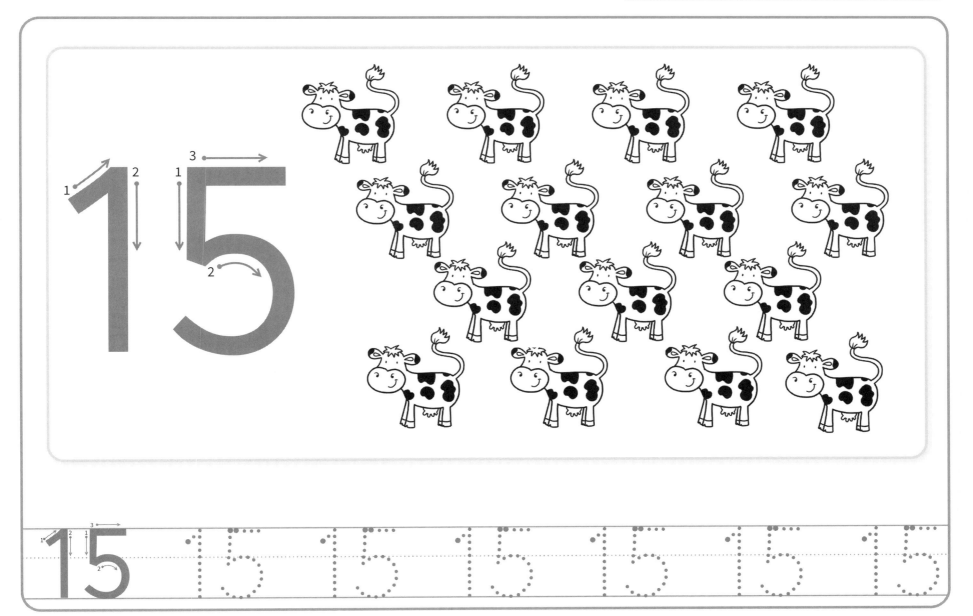

 **Count.** ◌ **Trace.** ✏ **Color.**

 **Count.** **Draw.** ◯ **Trace.**

Review the numbers. The children count the sheep and draw one more to complete 15. Repeat the procedure for the rabbits. Finally, they trace the numbers with different colored crayons.

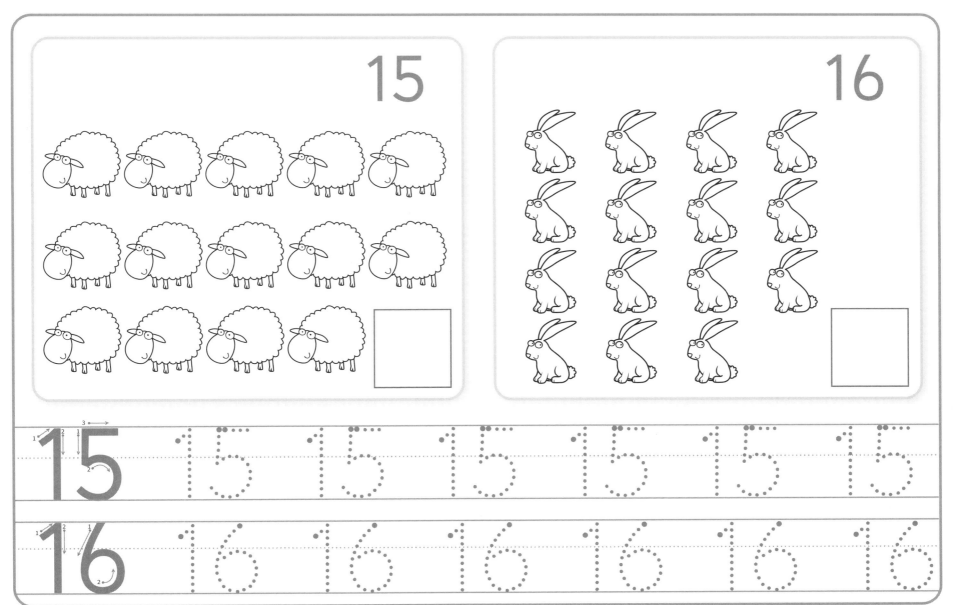

15

16

○ **Trace.** ✎ **Write.** ✏ **Color.**

 Present the letter. Then the children trace and write the letters with different colored crayons. Finally, they color the sun freely.

⭕ Trace. ✏️ Write. 🖌️ Paint.

○ **Trace.** ✎ **Write.** ✏ **Color.**

Present the letter. Then the children trace and write the letters with different colored crayons. Finally, they color the letter and the umbrella freely.

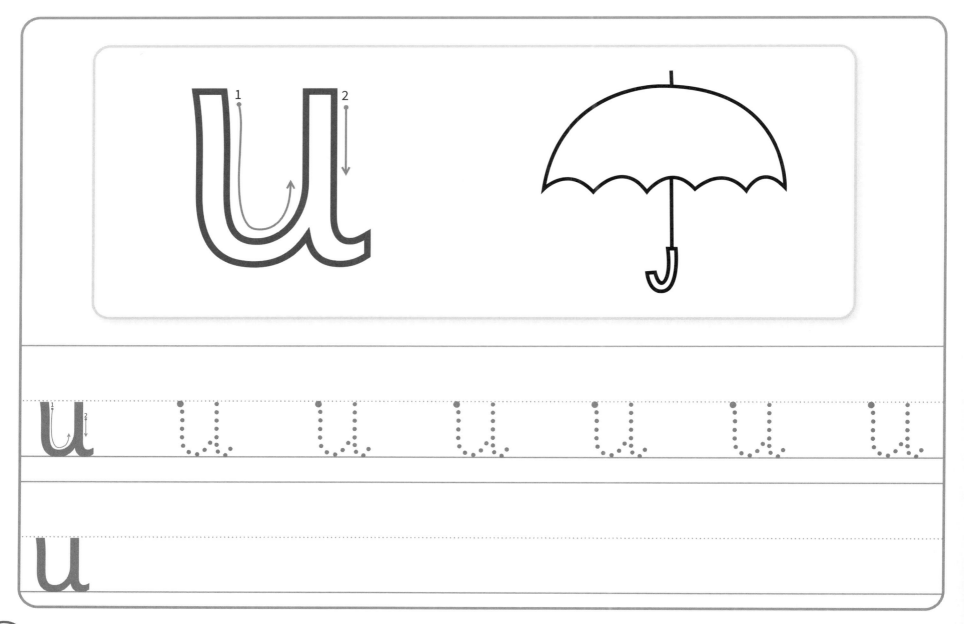

 **Count.** **Trace.** **Color.**

Present the number. Then the children count the pears and trace the numbers with different colored crayons. Finally, they color the pears freely.

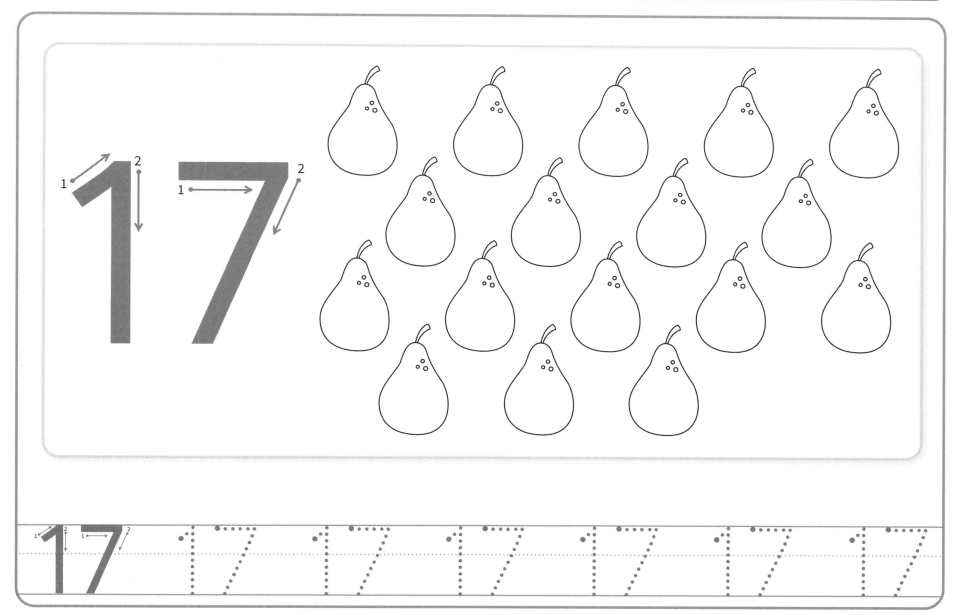

✋ Count. ⬭ Trace. ✏ Color.

👋 Count. ⚪ Trace. ✏️ Color.

Review the numbers. The children count the items of food in each set. Then they trace the numbers with different colored crayons. Finally, the children color the food freely.

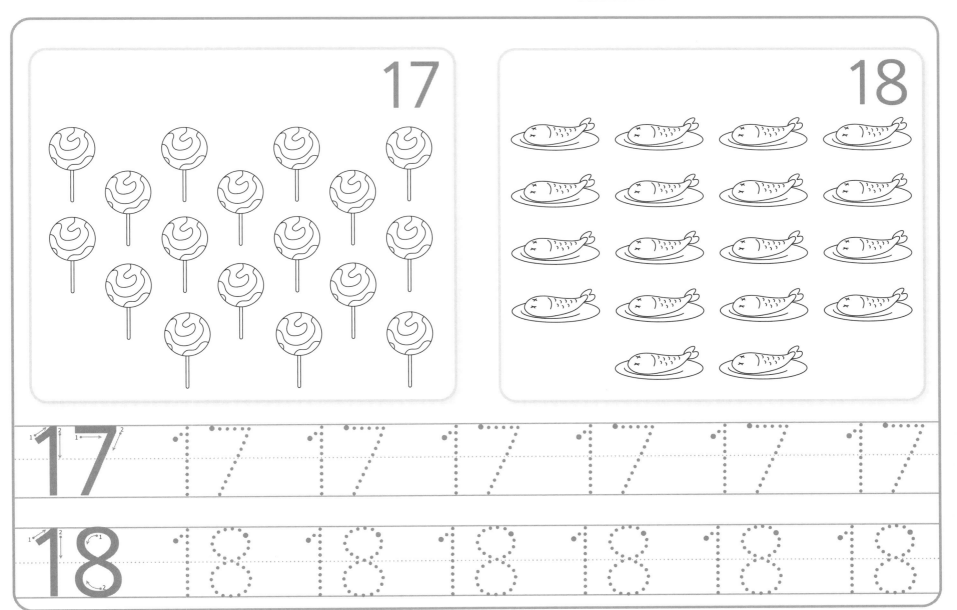

✏️ **Color.** ⭕ **Trace.** ✏️ **Write.**

Present the letter. Then the children color the picture of the word that starts with letter "v." Finally, they trace and write the letters with different colored crayons.

<u>v</u>an

<u>m</u>ouse

V v v v v v v

V

 **Color.** ⭕ **Trace.** ✏️ **Write.**

 Present the letter. Then the children identify and color the letters "w" in the box. Finally, they trace and write the letters with different colored crayons.

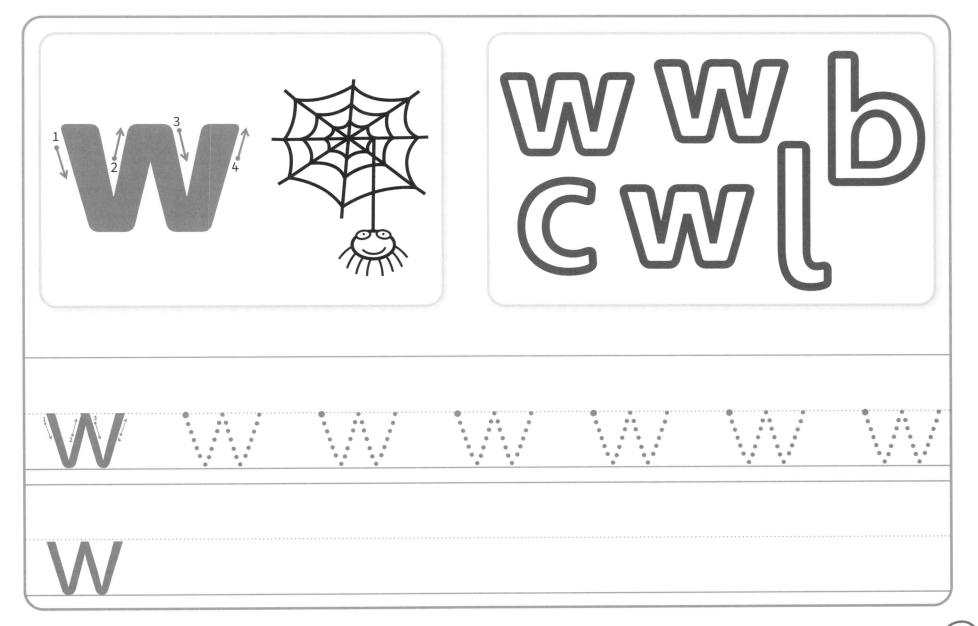

◯ Trace. ✎ Write. ✏ Color.

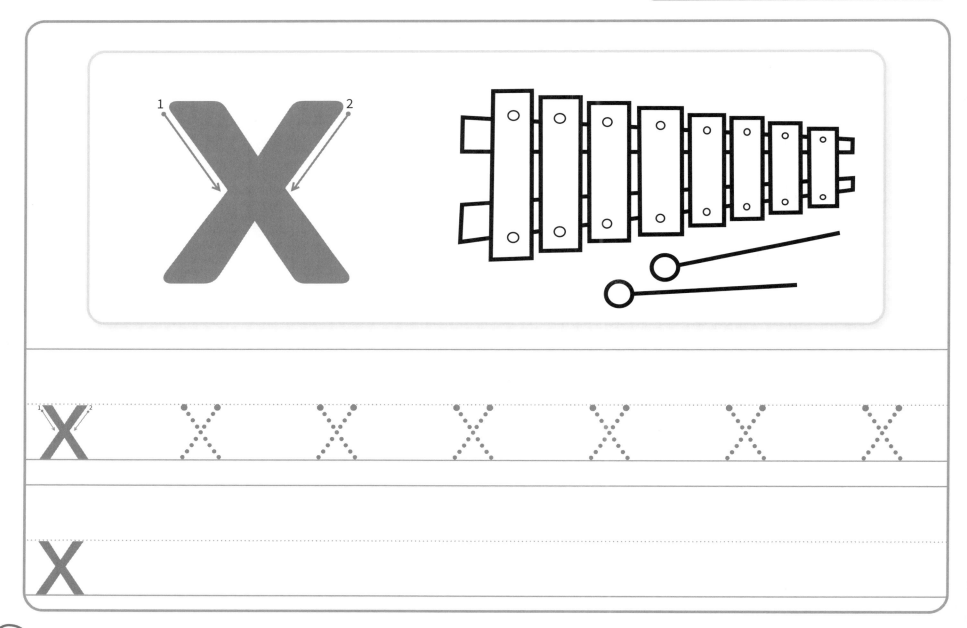

 **Count.** ⭕ **Trace.** ✏️ **Color.**

 **Count.** **Trace.** **Color.**

 Present the number. Then the children count the watermelons and trace the numbers with different colored crayons. Finally, they color the watermelons freely.

 **Count.** **Draw.** **Trace.**

 Review the numbers. Then the children identify the number 19 and draw the corresponding number of leaves in the box. Repeat the procedure for the number 20 and the watermelons. Finally, they trace the numbers with different colored crayons.

○ **Trace.** ✏ **Write.** 🖍 **Color.**

Present the letter. Then the children trace and write the letters on the lines. Finally, they color the picture freely.

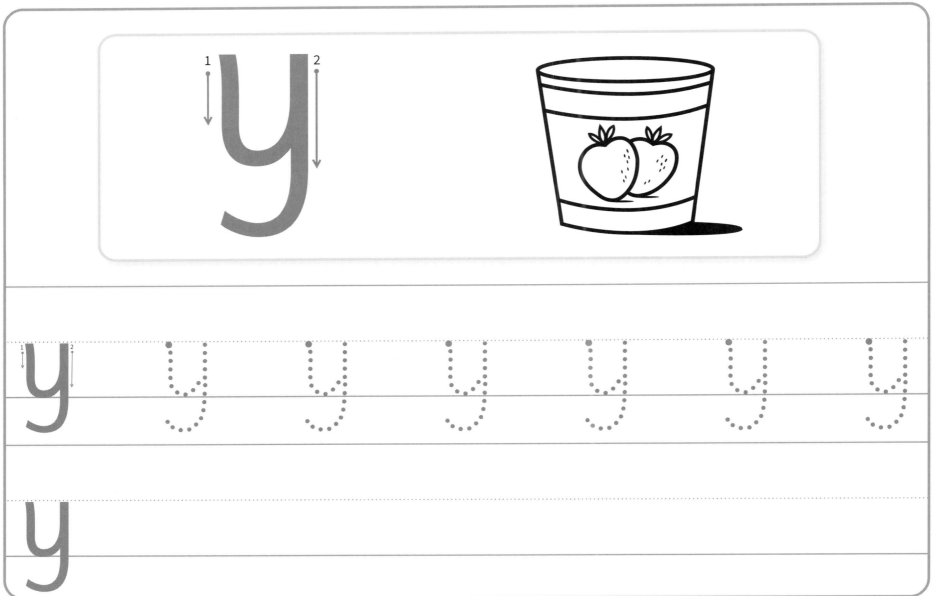

◯ Trace. ✏ Write. 🖌 Paint.

Present the letter. Then the children trace and write the letters with different colored crayons. Finally, they finger-paint the letter "z" and the zebra. Alternatively, they can color the letter and the zebra with crayons.

○ Trace. ✏ Color.

The children trace the letters with different colored crayons. Then they color the pictures freely.

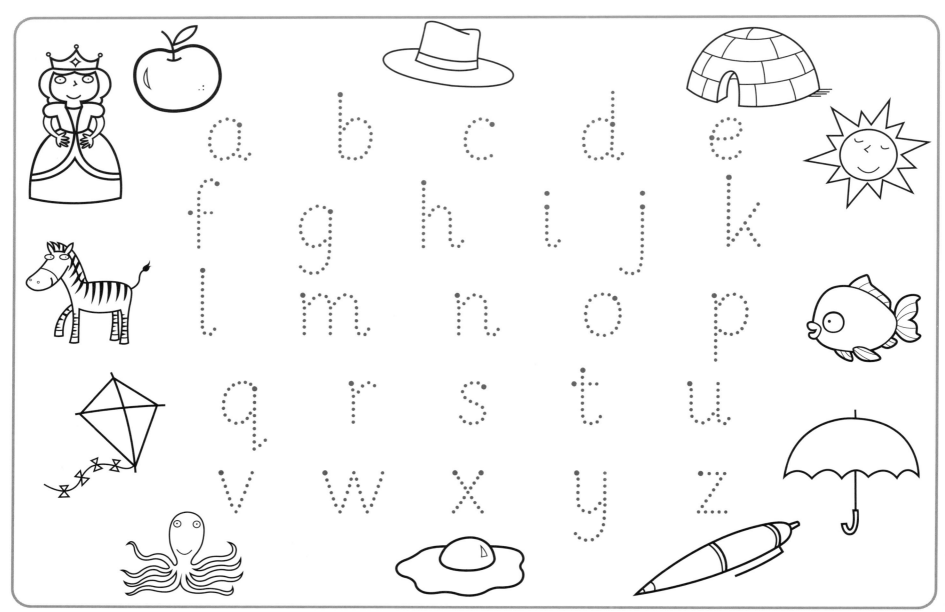

a b c d e

f g h i j k

l m n o p

q r s t u

v w x y z

 **Draw.** **Match.** **Color.**

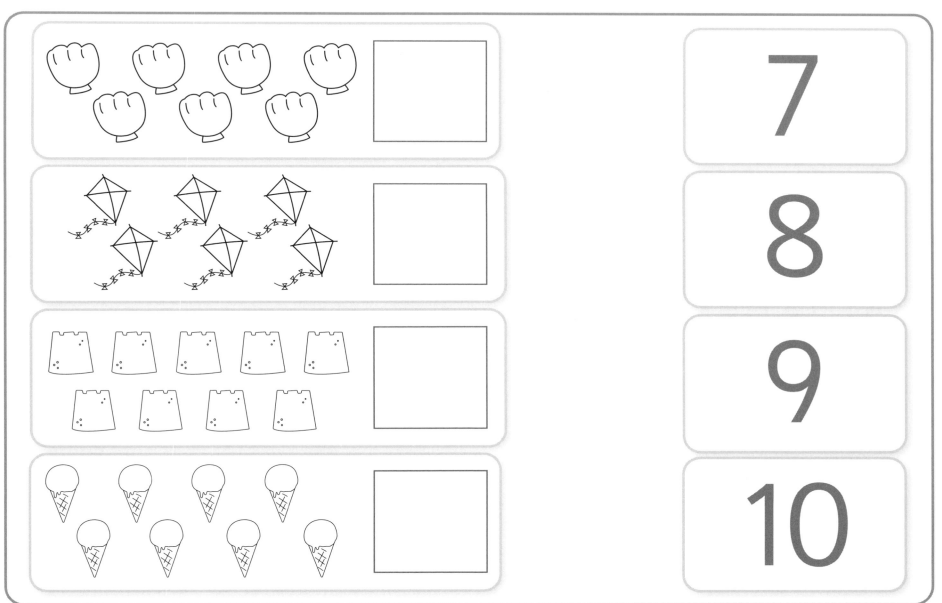

7

8

9

10

✋ Count. ⭕ Trace. ✏️ Color.

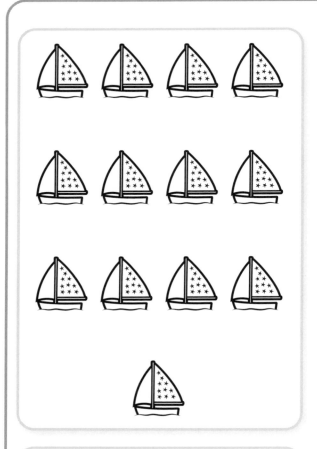

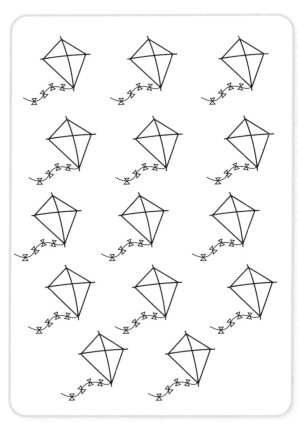

 **Count.** **Trace.**

The children count the lily pads aloud. Then they trace the numbers.

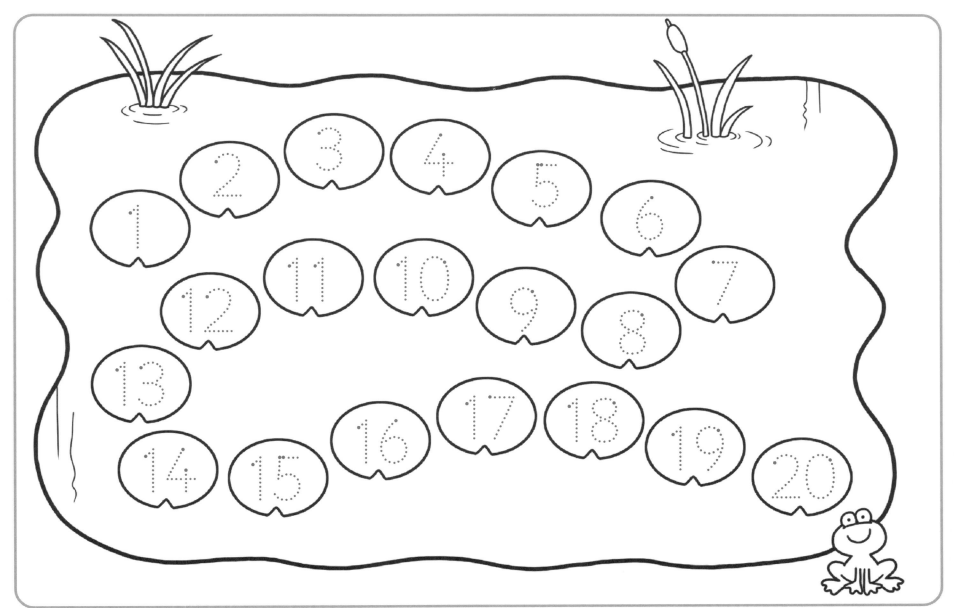

Thanks and acknowledgements

The publishers and authors would like to thank the following contributors:

Page make-up by Blooberry Design and QBS Learning.
Cover concept by Blooberry Design. Front cover photography by
NYS444/iStock/Getty Images.

Illustrations by Louise Gardner, Marek Jagucki, Sue King (Plum Pudding) and
Bernice Lum. Icons (color, count, draw, look, match, say, trace, tick, write) by
https://thenounproject.com/icon.